Shag

Follow us on Facebook: **Rainbow Coloring Books**
Add me on my personal FB: **Joe Ellison (http://bit.ly/1r31Bay)**
Instagram : **Rainbowcoloring**
or add us on Snapchat: **Rainbowcoloring**

Get free pages to enjoy and color, bonuses, discounts and a behind the scenes look at our process.

rainbowcoloring

DOWNLOAD THE DIGITAL PDF EDITION OF THIS BOOK FOR UNLIMITED PRINTING (3 Bonus Included)

Black Background : **http://bit.ly/28pPsNO**
White background : **http://bit.ly/1U4Tsz1**

REVIEWS ARE OUR OXYGEN AND HELPS US CREATE AWESOME BOOKS. WOULD YOU BE KIND ENOUGH TO LEAVE US A REVIEW ON AMAZON?

Swear Word Coloring Book

F*ck Off Coloring Book
Featuring Sweary Words, Animals and Flowers

Rainbow Coloring & Joe Ellison

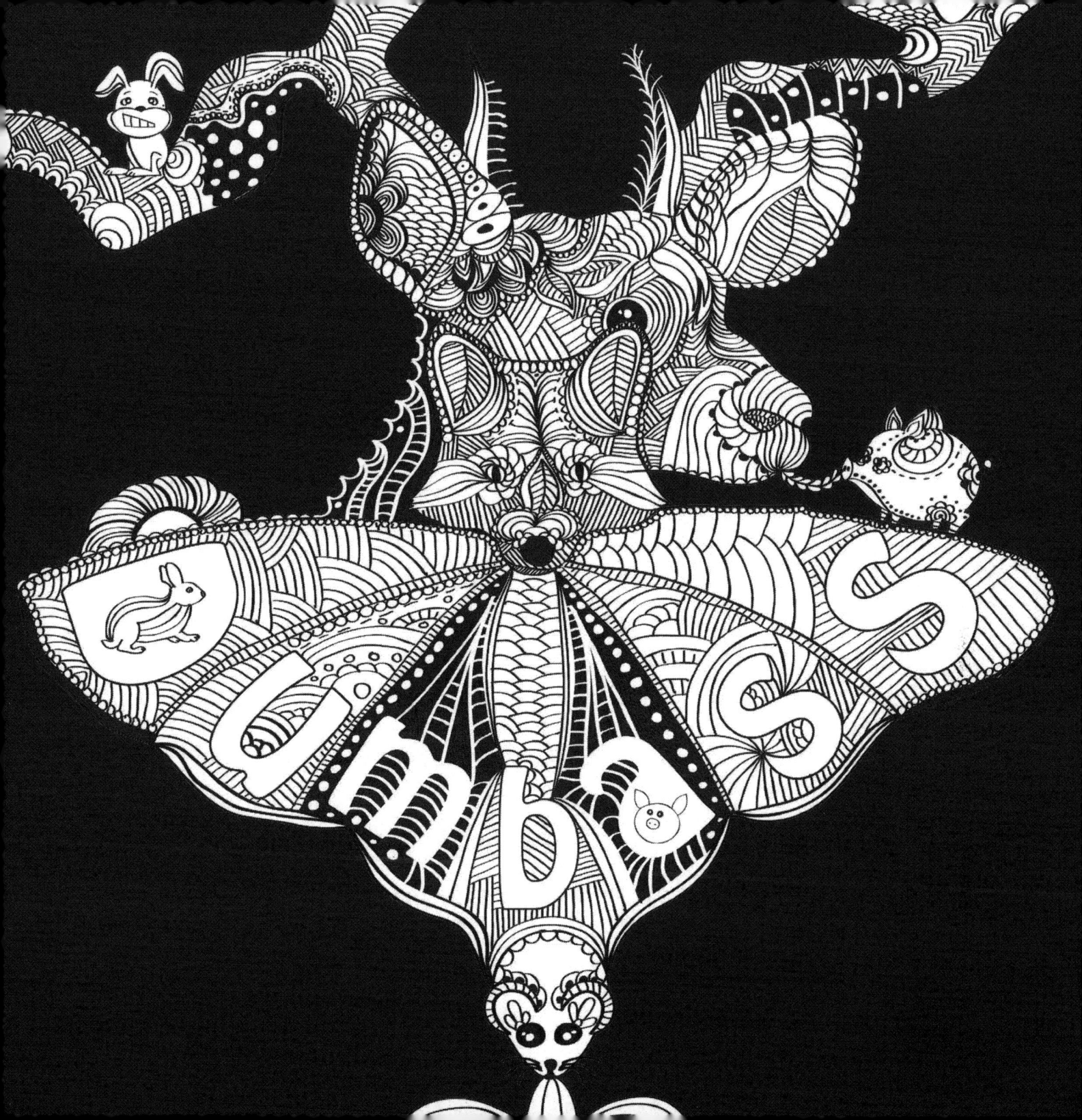

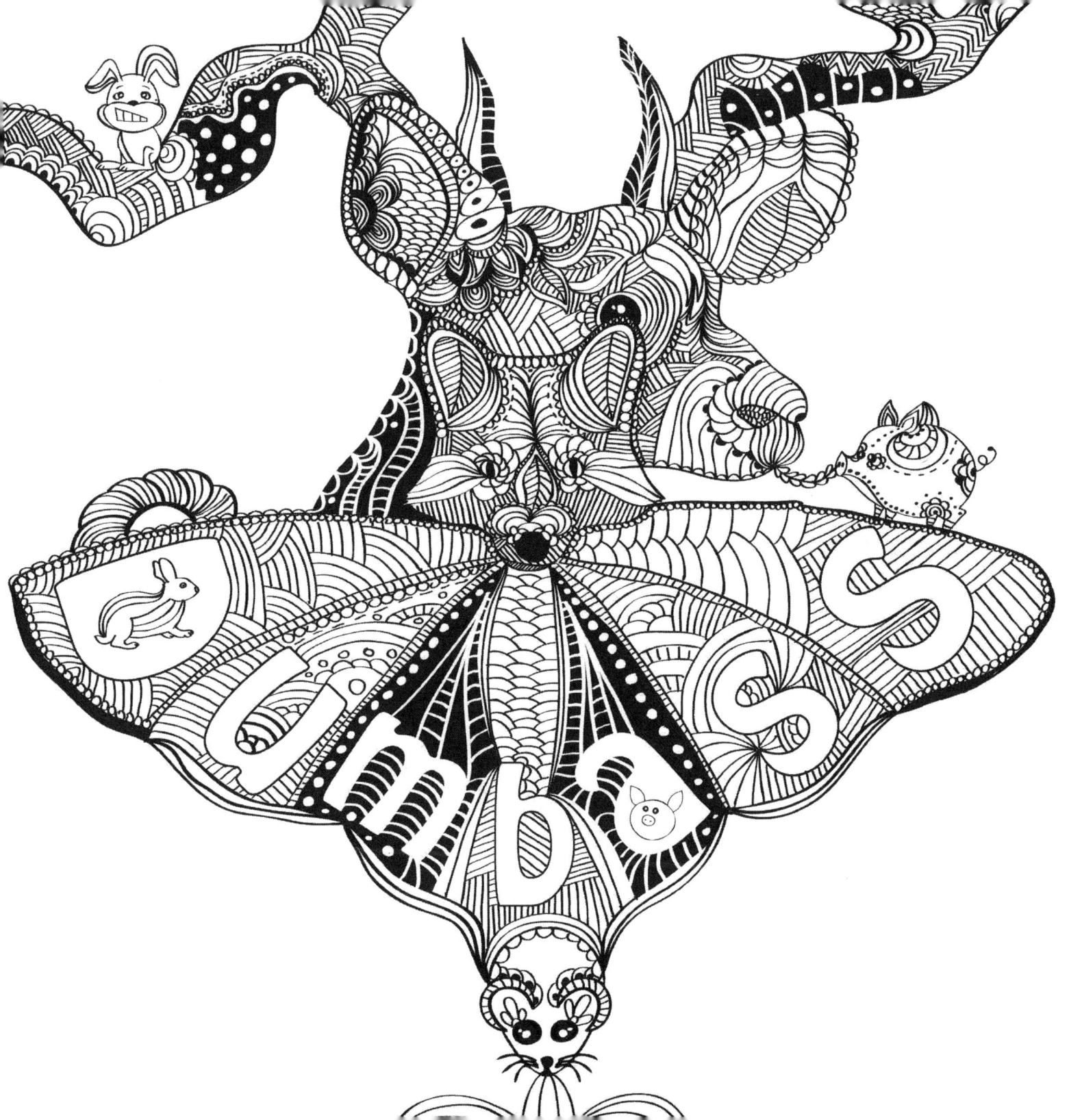

Printed in Great Britain
by Amazon